The Story of a Special Day
Volume 170

June

18

The 169th day of the year (170th in leap years). There are 196 days remaining until the end of the year.

by Michael Dobson

Timespinner
Press

This book is (or will be) available in e-book form for Kindland other formats from your favorite online booksellers.

For more information about the series, about us, or about your special day, please email us at editor@timespinnerpress.com.

Look for other volumes in *The Story of a Special Day*, coming often. See www.timespinnerpress.com for details and for the most recent information.

Table of Contents

Cover: *The Battle of Waterloo 1815*, by Thomas Jones Parker. The Battle of Waterloo took place on Sunday, June 18, 1815 — the **EVENT OF THE DAY**.

Quote of the Day

"Nothing except a battle lost can be half so melancholy as a battle won."

Arthur Wellesley, 1st Duke of Wellington
on the Battle of Waterloo, which took place on
Sunday, June 18, 1815

Today in History

June 18

Napoleon Bonaparte, by Paul Delaroche

Event of the Day
The Battle of Waterloo

On Sunday, June 18, 1815, French troops led by Napoleon Bonaparte met two opposing armies, one British and one Prussian, near the town of Waterloo, then part of the Netherlands and now in Belgium. The Battle of Waterloo ended the reign of Napoleon and reshaped the face of Europe.

Napoleon came to power in the dangerous days following the 1789 French Revolution. The execution of King Louis XVI and overthrow of the old nobility deeply worried other European monarchs, who feared that these republican sentiments would spread. They attempted to destroy the fledgling French Republic, but instead, French forces ended up victorious. One of their best military commanders, Napoleon Bonaparte, quickly rose in stature through his brilliant conquests of Italy and Egypt.

Conflict between the ruling Directorate and the increasingly powerful Napoleon led to a 1799 coup d'état and a new constitution that named Napoleon "First Consul." It was nominally democratic, but in fact Napoleon held near total power.

After several assassination attempts and plots aimed at returning the Bourbon family to the throne of France, Napoleon decided that a Roman-style monarchy (with himself as monarch) would make a Bourbon restoration difficult. He crowned himself Napoleon I, Emperor of the French, in 1804.

During this entire period, peace was a rarity. European leaders still wanted to crush the French, but the French weren't cooperating. Soon, Napoleon dominated most of Europe, capturing cities as far asway as Vienna. While the French by no means won every battle, they were overall remarkably successful.

That is, until Napoleon decided to invade Russia. Of an invading force of more than 400 thousand front-line troops, only 40,000 returned, survivors of the Russian winter. Severely weakened, Napoleon was unable to defeat a seven-nation coalition. In April 2014, he abdicated the throne as part of the peace treaty, and was exiled to the Mediterranean island of Elba. He did not stay long.

In February 1815, he escaped with a small force of 700 men. The first French regiment sent to intercept him instead came over to his side, and soon he was once again the commander of the armies of France.

The anti-Napoleon Seventh Coalition,the United Kingdom, Russia, Austria, and Prussia, met at the Congress of Vienna and declared Napoleon an outlaw. Napoleon quickly realized that he could not fight them all together, and decided to attack before his opponents were ready. British forces and Prussian forces wer already beginning to mobilize in Brussels. If Napoleon could only destroy them before reinforcements arrived, he might be able to drive the British back to the sea and drive the Prussians out of the war long enough for him to fully rebuild his own forces.

Arthur Wellesley, 1st Duke of Wellington, by Thomas Lawrence
Commanded British forces at the Battle of Waterloo

Gebhard Leberecht von Blücher
Commanded Prussian forces at the Battle of Waterloo

Napoleon's forces consisted of some 73,000 men. Together, the British and Prussians had 118,000. As Napoleon crossed into enemy territory, his forces easily overran Coalitiion outposts and he moved toward the center. In early engagements at Quatre Bras and Ligny, Coalition forces were pushed back.

Finally, on the evening of June 17, the British commander, Arthur Wellesley, the first Duke of Wellington, decided to hold his ground near Waterloo. The Prussian army, commanded by Field Marshal Gebhard von Blücher, was only eight miles away, and would join the British in the morning.

None of the combatants were in the best of condition. Although the French had fierce and loyal fighters, they had force-marched through rain and black coal dust, and had little food. Wellington said the British were "an infamous army, very weak and ill-equipped, and a very inexperienced Staff." He was short on cavalry and guns. The Prussians were in the middle of a major reorganization when they began to march, and some of its elements lacked equipment and training.

Wellington woke up at around 2 am, and wrote letters till dawn, when he began issuing orders to deploy his forces. Prussian forces began to march toward Waterloo, but heavy rain had made the roads muddy and congested. Meanwhile, Napoleon had breakfast on silver plates and announced to his generals, "Wellington is a bad general, the English are bad troops, and this affair is nothing more than eating breakfast." (Napoleon believed praising the enemy was bad for morale.)

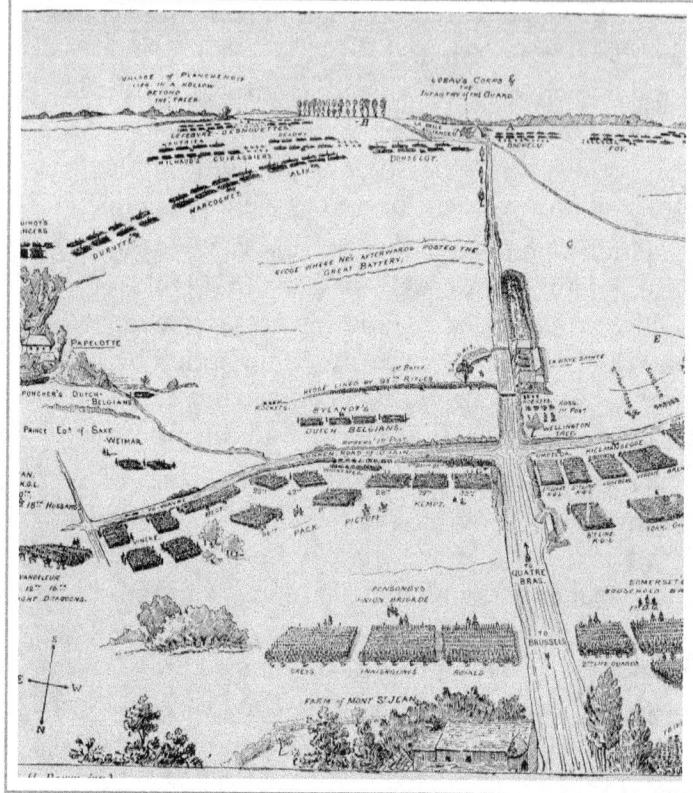

A map of the Battle of Waterloo, from *Battles of the Nineteenth*

The actual battle began late that morning and raged until nearly ten at night with the final defeat of the French forces. Engagements were fought along an area nearly fifty miles wide. At different times during the day the advantage was held by one side or another. Wellington later said that Waterloo was "the nearest-run thing you ever saw in your life."

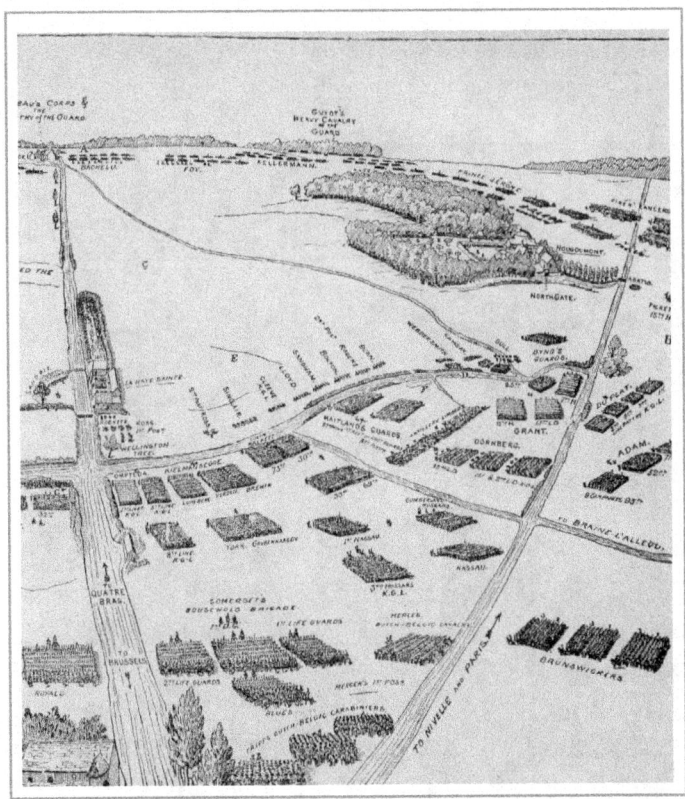

Century, by Archibald Forbes and A. Hilliard Atteridge (1901)

By battle's end, Wellington lost 15,000 men and Blücher 7,000. Napoleon lost between 24,000 and 26,000, as well as 6,000 to 7,000 captured and an additional 15,000 desertions following the defeat. Napoleon abdicated for a second time on June 24, and was exiled to the South Atlantic island of Saint Helena, one of the most remote islands in the world, where he lived out his remaining days.

Amelia Earhart prior to her 1928 transatlantic flight

What Happened on June 18?

From the creation of great works of engineering and art, to devastating wars and natural disasters, thousands of years of history have left their mark on each and every day of the year. Here are some important events that occurred on June 18. (Illustrated items are boxed.)

618 — The **Tang Dynasty** comes to power in China with the accession of Emperor Gaozu (唐高祖) to the imperial throne. It would rule for nearly 300 years and the period was considered a golden age in Chinese civilization.

1429 — French forces under the overall leadership of **Joan of Arc** defeat a large British army at the Battle of Patay, turning the tide of the Hundred Years' War.

1812 — The **War of 1812** officially begins with a US declaration of war against Great Britain.

1928 — **Amelia Earhart** becomes the first woman to be flown (as a passenger) across the Atlantic Ocean. She will later become the first woman to make a solo transatlantic flight as pilot.

1940 — In the "Appeal of 18 June," Free French leader Charles de Gaulle creates the **French Resistance** to Nazi occupation during World War II in one of the most famous radio address in French history.

1940 — British Prime Minister **Winston Churchill** gives his "This was their finest hour" speech before the House of Commons.

1981 — The first operational **stealth fighter,** the Lockheed F-117 Nighthawk, makes its first flight.

1983 — Space Shuttle astronaut **Sally Ride** becomes the first American woman in space.

2006 — The nation of **Kazakhstan launches its first satellite** into Earth orbit.

Astronaut Sally Ride aboard the Space Shuttle *Challenger*

Winston Churchill

Quote of the Day

"And in the end, the love you take is equal to the love you make."

Paul McCartney,
singer-songwriter, member of The Beatles
born June 18, 1942

Births

and

Deaths

June 18

Paul McCartney with The Beatles (Courtesy Beeld en Geluid).
McCartney was born June 18, 1942.

Notable June 18 People

With the current world population at about seven billion people, on average about 19 million people also celebrate their birthdays on June 18 — and that isn't counting the millions and millions who came before! No matter when you were born, you share your birthday with many special people whose accomplishments (and occasionally embarrassments) have been noted as part of history.

In this section, you'll meet fascinating people who share your birthday. They're organized by what they're famous for, and then in reverse chronological order from most recent to earliest. Those who are shown in photographs or artwork have a box around them. We don't have photos of everyone, so please forgive us if your favorite person is missing.

Some of these people you've heard of, others may be new to you, but they all make up an important part of the reason that June 18 is a truly special day!

Uncle Sam Wants You, by James Montgomery Flagg

Who Was Born on June 18?

Adventure

Red Adair, legendary oil well firefighter, subject of the 1968 John Wayne film *Hellfighters*. *(1915)*

Art and Illustration

James Montgomery Flagg, artist best known for his World War I era "Uncle Sam Wants You!" poster. *(1877)*

Business and Economics

Barack Obama, Sr., Kenyan economist and father of the 44th President of the United States. *(1936)*

Philip Crosby, best-selling management author who pioneered the "zero defects" approach to quality management. *(1926)*

Franco Modigliani, won the 1985 Nobel Memorial Prize in Economics for his work in understanding corporate finance and national savings. *(1918)*

Sylvia Porter, economist and writer of numerous best-selling books and newspaper columns, with a readership of as many as 40 million people. *(1913)*

Henry Folger, president and chairman of Standard Oil of New York and Shakespeare collector; founded the Folger Shakespeare Library. *(1857)*

E. W. Scripps, newspaper publisher and media tycoon who founded what later became United Press International (UPI). *(1854)*

Food

Delia Smith, UK's best-selling cookery author and television personality. *(1941)*

Robert Mondavi, winemaker who helped California wines gain recognition and sales worldwide. *(1913)*

Government and Military

Uday Hussein (عُدي صدّام حُسين), son and presumed heir of Iraqi dictator Saddam Hussein, killed following the US-led invasion of Iraq. *(1964)*

Tibor Rubin, Hungarian born Holocaust survivor who emigrated to the United States and received the Medal of Honor during the Korean War. *(1929)*

Grand Duchess Anastasia of Russia, youngest daughter of the last tsar of Russia, killed along with her family during the Communist takeover of that country but rumored to have survived. Her supposed survival and subsequent life have been dramatized in several movies, including the 1956 Ingrid Bergman film *Anastasia*, and the 1997 Disney animated film of the same name. It has since been proved that she did not survive. *(1901 [O.S.* June 5])*

* Russia only switched to the Gregorian calendar in 1918, well after the rest of Europe. Our June 18 is equivalent to "Old Style" June 5. For more, see "What Day of the Week is June 18?"

Grand Duchess Anastasia *(standing)* with her sister Maria

Hélène Napoleone Bonaparte, reputed daughter of Napoleon by his mistress, born during his exile to Saint Helena. Although Napoleon never officially acknowledged her, she is said to have looked very much like him. What happened to her after her exile is unknown. *(1816)*

Robert Stewart, Viscount Castlereagh, British foreign secretary during the Napoleonic wars, responsible for managing the anti-Napoleon coalition. *(1769)*

Journalism

Roger Ebert, newspaper columnist who became the first film critic to win a Pulitzer Prize, co-host (with Gene Siskel) of the PBS series *Sneak Previews. (1942)*

Roger Ebert

Music

Blake Shelton, country musician with seven Grammy nominations, best known for such hits as "Austin" and "All Over Me." *(1976)*

Dizzy Reed, musician best known as the keyboardist for the rock band Guns N' Roses. *(1963)*

Paul McCartney, singer-songwriter and multi-instrumentalist who gained fame as a member of The Beatles, two-time inductee into the Rock and Roll Hall of Fame, and a 21-time Grammy winner whose song "Yesterday" has been covered by more artists than any other copyrighted song in history. *(1942)* *(Photo page 20.)*

Sammy Cahn, songwriter who won four Academy Awards, known for such hits as "Let it Snow!," "High Hopes," "Call Me Irresponsible," and many more. *(1913)*

Performing Arts

Isabella Rossellini, actress and filmmaker known for such films as *Blue Velvet* and *Death Becomes Her,* daughter of actress Ingrid Bergman. *(1952)*

Carol Kane, actress best known for playing the wife of Latka in the 1980s sitcom *Taxi,* for which she won two Emmy Awards. *(1952)*

Linda Thorson, actress best known for playing Tara King in the television series *The Avengers. (1947)*

Paul Eddington, actor known for his roles in the British sitcoms *The Good Life* and *Yes Minister/Yes Prime Minister. (1927)*

Ian Carmichael, British actor best known for playing the Dorothy Sayers character Lord Peter Wimsey on television and radio. *(1920)*

Richard Boone, actor who starred in the television series *Have Gun — Will Travel. (1917)*

Richard Boone as Paladin from *Have Gun — Will Travel* (1962)

E. G. Marshall, actor best known for his roles in the 1960s and 1970s television shows *The Defenders* and *The Bold Ones,* also known for his role as "Juror #4" in the 1957 courtroom drama *12 Angry Men.* *(1914)*

Bud Collyer, pioneering host of television game shows such as *Beat the Clock* and *To Tell the Truth,* voice of Clark Kent/Superman on radio and in animated shorts. *(1908)*

Keye Luke (陸錫麒), Chinese-American actor best known for playing "Number One Son" in the *Charlie Chan* film series and Master Po in the 1970s television series *Kung Fu.* *(1904)*

Jeanette MacDonald, starred in numerous 1930s musicals, famous for her partnerships with Nelson Eddy and Maurice Chevalier. *(1903)*

Lobby card of Clark Gable and **Jeanette MacDonald** from the 1936 film *San Francisco*

Science and Medicine

Dudley Herschbach, shared the 1986 Nobel Prize in Chemistry for work on the dynamics of chemical elementary proceesses. *(1932)*

Jerome Karle, shared the 1985 Nobel Prize in Chemistry for his work in the analysis of crystal structures using X-ray scattering. *(1918)*

Charles Laveran, won the 1907 Nobel Prize in Physiology or Medicine for discovering the causative agents of malaria and other diseases. *(1845)*

Sports

Bruce Smith, defensive end for the Buffalo Bills and Washington Redskins, member of the Pro Football Hall of Fame. *(1963)*

Lou Brock, left fielder for the St. Louis Cardinals known for setting a new major league stolen base record, member of the Baseball Hall of Fame. *(1939)*

George Mikan, pioneer of professional basketball, member of the Naismith Memorial Basketball Hall of Fame and selected as one of the NBA's 50 greatest players of all time. *(1924)*

Glenn Morris, track and field athlete who set a world record in winning the gold medal in decathalon in the 1936 Olympics, played Tarzan in the 1938 film *Tarzan's Revenge*. *(1912)*

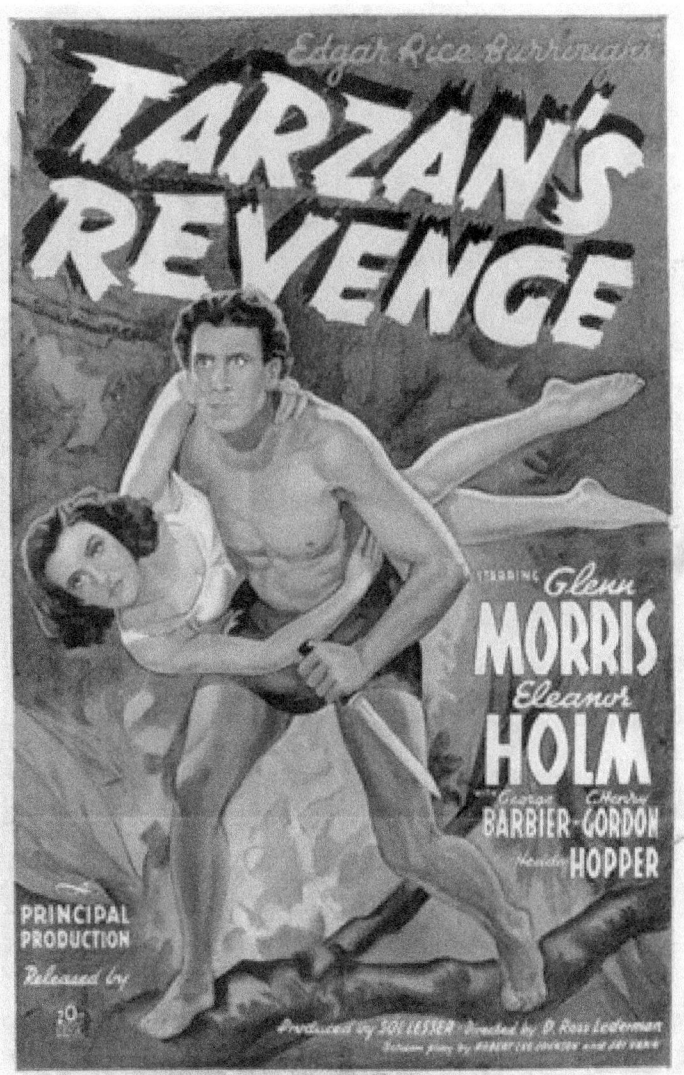

Poster from the 1938 film *Tarzan's Revenge*, starring **Glenn Morris**

Roald Amundsen, by Daniel Georg Nyblin
(Courtesy National Library of Norway)

Who Died on June 18?

Exploration

Roald Amundsen, Norwegian explorer known as the first person to have reached both the North and South Poles. *(1928†)*

Government and Politics

Yelena Bonner (Еле́на Бо́ннэр), human rights activist and dissident in the Soviet Union, wife of dissident physicist Andrei Sakharov. *(2011)*

Journalism

I.F. Stone, American investigative journalist best known as the editor and publisher of the eponymous *I.F. Stone's Weekly. (1989)*

Alan Berg, liberal talk radio host in Denver, Colorado, assassinated by the white nationalist group The Order; his story inspired the films *Betrayed* and *Talk Radio. (1984)*

---

† Amundsen and five crewmen died on a rescue mission in the Arctic on June 18, 1928, when their plane went down. It's most likely they were killed in the crash, but no bodies were recovered.

Literature

José Saramago, Portuguese writer who won the 1998 Nobel Prize in Literature. *(2010)*

John Cheever, American novelist known as "the Chekhov of the suburbs," winner of the National Medal for Literature and the Pulitzer Prize for Fiction. *(1982)*

Djuna Barnes, writer and artist best known for her 1936 novel *Nightwood*, known both for her contributions to lesbian fiction and to the modernist school of writing. *(1982)*

Maxim Gorky (Макси́м Го́рькій), Russian writer who helped found the socialist realism school; nominated five times for the Nobel Prize in Literature. *(1936)*

Samuel Butler, British author best known for his utopian satire *Erewhon* and a posthumously published novel *The Way of All Flesh*. *(1902)*

Tom Brown, English satirist remembered primarily for a four line insult aimed at one of his Oxford professors, "I do not love thee, Dr. Fell / The reason why I cannot tell / But this I know, and know full well / I do not love thee, Dr. Fell." *(1704)*

Military

Georgy Zhukov (Гео́ргий Жу́ков), Soviet military leader who served as Chief of the General Staff and Minister of Defense during and following World War II. *(1974)*

Simon Bolivar Buckner, Jr., American lieutenant general who led the amphibious assault on Okinawa during World War II; highest-ranking US officer lost to enemy fire in that war. *(1945)*

Max Immelmann, German fighter ace in World War I with 15 victories, known for developing the airplane maneuver known as the Immelmann turn. *(1916)*

Lakshmibal, the Rani of Jhansi, queen of a state in north-central India, a central figure of the 1857 Indian Rebellion and a national symbol of resistance to the British Raj. *(1858)*

The Rani of Jhansi, dressed as a cavalrywoman

Thomas Picton, British lieutenant general who was the highest-ranking officer killed at the Battle of Waterloo; the Duke of Wellington called him "a rough foul-mouthed devil as ever lived." *(1815)*

Music

Clarence Clemons, saxophone player best known as a member of Bruce Springsteen's E Street Band. *(2011)*

Clarence Clemons with the E Street Band in 2009.
(Photo: Jamison Foser, CC BY-SA 2.0.)

Performing Arts

Phil Austin, comedian and writer best known as a member of the surrealistic comedy group The Firesign Theatre. *(2015)*

Nancy Marchand, actress best known for portraying Margaret Pynchon on the television series *Lou Grant,* and Livia Soprano on *The Sopranos. (2000)*

Thomas Gomez, first Hispanic-American nominated for an Academy Award for the 1947 film *Ride the Pink Horse. (1971)*

Ethel Barrymore, actress known as the "First Lady of the American Theater," won an Academy Award for the 1944 film *None but the Lonely,* member of the Barrymore family of actors. *(1959)*

Science

Stephanie Kwolek, chemist who developed Kevlar, member of the National Inventors Hall of Fame. *(2014)*

Paul Karrer, shared the 1937 Nobel Prize for Chemistry for his research on vitamins. *(1971)*

Sports

Larry Doby, baseball player with the Negro Leagues who became the second black player to break the color barrier and join Major League Baseball; member of the Baseball Hall of Fame. *(2003)*

1951 Bowman Gum trading card of Larry Doby

Quote of the Day

"'Kindness' covers all of my political
beliefs. No need to spell them out. I believe
that if, at the end, according to our abilities,
we have done something to make others a
little happier, and something to make
ourselves a little happier, that is about the
best we can do."

Roger Ebert, film critic
born June 18, 1942

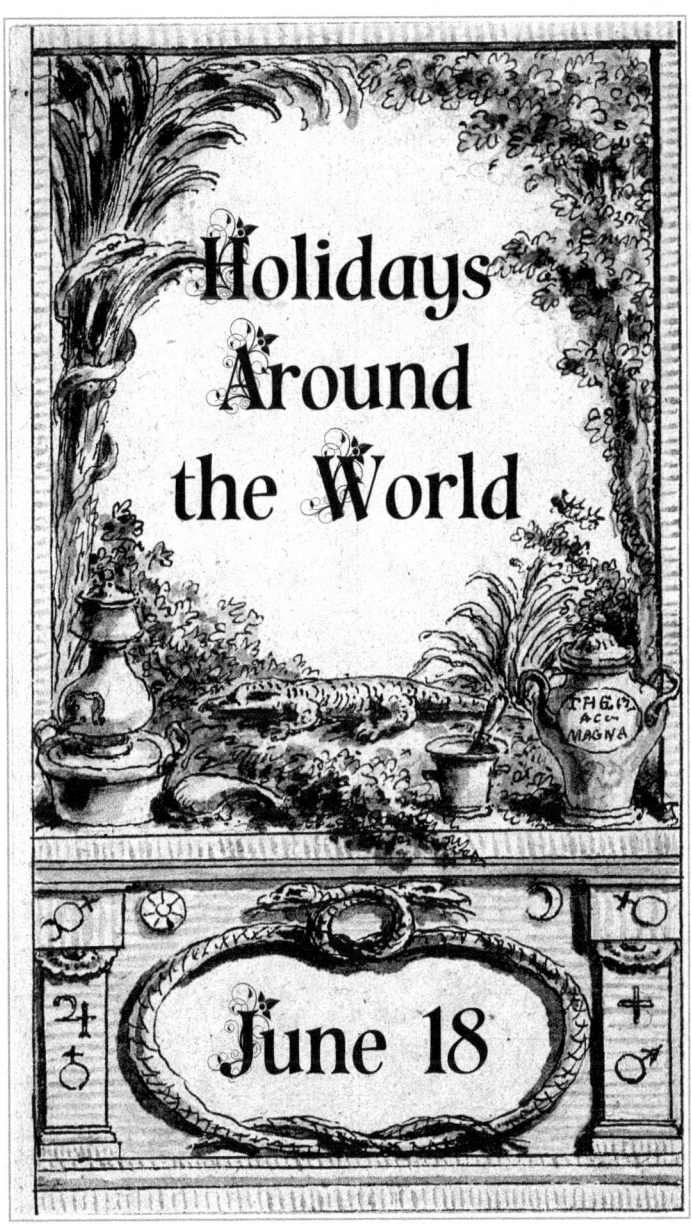

Holidays
Around
the World

June 18

Poster for a 1940 Father and Son Banquet by Albert M. Bender, for Father's Day. (Works Projects Adminstration Poster Collection)

Holidays Around the World

If you're looking for a reason to take your special day off, you should know that every single day is a holiday somewhere in the world! Here's some of what you can celebrate on June 18!

Father's Day (US, date varies)

Father's Day is celebrated in many countries around the world, but the date varies. The custom originated in Catholic Europe in the Middle Ages, where it is still celebrated on St. Joseph's Day, March 19. Joseph was the earthly father of Jesus, and thus Father's Day came into being.

Father's Day first reached the New World via Spain and Portugal, so most Latin American countries also celebrate on March 19. Coptic Christian in Egypt and North Africa use July 20.

In the United States, Mother's Day came first, with a 1908 celebration in West Virginia. By 1914, President Woodrow Wilson made it a national holiday observed on the second Sunday in May. The first attempt to create a corresponding Father's Day was in 1910.

Although unofficial observance of the day was common by the 1930s, it wasn't until 1966 that the first Presidential Proclamation of the day was issued, and until 1972 it became an annual holiday by law, held on the third Sunday in June. That means in the US Father's Day can occur on any day between June 15 and June 21 each year.

Fixed Celebrations

- **Araw ng Pagkakatatag ng Benguet** (Benguet Foundation Day, Benguet, Philippines)
- **Autistic Pride Day** (international)
- **Human Rights Day** (Azerbaijan)
- **National Day** (Seychelles)
- **Queen Mother's Birthday** (honors the birthday of Queen Mother Norodom Monineath in 1936, Cambodia)
- **Waterloo Day** (celebrated by certain regiments of the British Army).

Moveable and Multi-Day Events

Some events take place over a specific week or time period. Start and finish dates may vary from year to year. Some events occur on different days each year (such as "fourth Saturday" of a given month). These events sometimes take place on June 18.

Second Thursday
- Seersucker Thursday (United States)

A Saturday

- Queen's Official Birthday (United Kingdom) (precise week varies)

HM Queen Elizabeth II inspects the line in the Trooping of the Color, part of the **QUEEN'S OFFICIAL BIRTHDAY** celebration.

Second Saturday

- Start of National Dairy Goat Awareness Week, ending on the third Saturday
- National Day (Montserrat, Pitcairn Islands, Saint Helena, South Georgia and South Sandwich Islands, Tristan da Cunha (United Kingdom))

Second Sunday

- Canadian Rivers Day
- Children's Day (United States)
- Father's Day (Austria, Belgium)
- Mother's Day (Luxembourg)
- Multicultural American Child Day
- Race Unity Day

Monday before US Father's Day

- International Men's Health Week: (Begins on the Monday before Father's Day, ends on Father's Day (United States)

Monday after the second Saturday

- Queen's Official Birthday (Norfolk Island)

Second Monday

- Queen's Official Birthday (Papua New Guinea, Solomon Islands, Australia, with the exception of Western Australia, which celebrates on the first Monday)

Religious Feast Days and Holidays

Every religion normally has feast days and holidays associated with it. While some religious days take place on a given calendar day, others occur on different days each year, usually because the date is determined by the phases of the Moon rather than the Earth's path around the Sun. Here are some religious feasts, festivals, and holidays that sometimes or always fall on June 18!

Saint Days

Each day in the year is considered a feast day for one or more saints. They are somewhat different in western Christianity (Catholicism and many forms of Protestantism) and in eastern (Orthodox) Christianity.

In **Western Christianity,** June 18 is the feast day of Saints Bernard Mizeki (Anglican and Episcopal Church), Elisabeth of Schönau, Gregorio Barbarigo, Leontius, Hypatius, and Theodolus.

In **Eastern Orthodox Christianity,** it is also the commemoration of three other Saint Leontiuses — the clairvoyant of Dionysiou, Leontius of the Kiev Caves, and Leontius the Shepherd. (These saints are honored on June 5 by Old Calendrists.‡)

In **Coptic Orthodox Christianity,** which uses its own calendar, June 18 is the equivalent of the 11th day of the month of Paoni. They commemorate Marina the Monk, as does the Maronite Church.

Celebrations About Food

In the United States, almost every day of the year is dedicated to a particular food. (Some other countries also have official food days, but only in America is there one every single day!) Sponsored by manufacturers, retailers, farmers, or simply fans, these days are often proclaimed by the President, Congress, state governors, or mayors. Given that there are more different foods than days of the year, some days honor more than one kind of food!

Some foods just get a day, while others get a whole month. Here's what to eat on June 18 and the rest of the month of June!

June 18 is...

- International Sushi Day
- International Picnic Day
- Insalata Day (for dishes based on vegetables)
- National Cheesmakers Day (US)

---

‡ "Old Calendrists" use the Julian, rather than the Gregorian, calendar. For an explanation of different calendar types, see "What Day of the Week is June 18?"

Sarah Vaughn, by William P. Gottlieb — for AFRICAN-AMERICAN
MUSIC APPRECIATION MONTH

The whole month of June is set aside to honorthe following foods.

- Georgia Blueberry Month
- National Candy Month
- National Dairy Month
- National Fresh Fruit and Vegetables Month
- National Iced Tea Month
- National Papaya Month

Honorary Months

Presidents, Congresses, and nations around the world issue proclamations recognizing particular months to honor certain causes. These events generally fall in April, though honorary months do come and go.

Holidays established by states and nonprofit organizations are listed if verified. If not otherwise specified, all months are US. There is some variation from year to year; some celebratory months get added and others get dropped. Two places to get up to date information are the current edition of Chase's Calendar of Events *or the website Brownielocks. Here are some honorary designations for June.*

- Adopt-a-Cat Month

- African-American Music Appreciation Month

- Bicycle Month (May 25 to June 25) (Canada)
- Caribbean American Heritage Month
- Children's Awareness Month

- Crop over (Barbados), celebrated until the first Monday in August.
- Dairy Alternative Month
- Fireworks Safety Month
- Gay and Lesbian Pride Month (US)
- Great Outdoors Month (US)
- International Surf Music Month
- Men's Health Education and Awareness Month
- National Accordion Awareness Month
- National Camping Month
- National Rivers Month
- National Safety Month
- National Smile Month (UK)
- National Oceans Month (United States)
- Season of Emancipation (April 14 to August 23) (Barbados)
- Women's Golf Month
- World Naked Bike Ride Month (northern hemisphere)

Just for Fun

Anybody can make up a holiday, and many people do! While none of these are officially recognized and some may come and go, here are a few more holidays for June 18.

- Go Fishing Day

- International Panic Day
- National Splurge Day

The Happy Moment, by James Goodwyn Clonney
for **GO FISHING DAY**

Quote of the Day

"Do you recall that night in June
Upon the Danube River;
We listened to the ländler-tune,
We watched the moonbeams quiver."

— Charles A. Aïdé, "Danube River"

About
the
Month
of

June

June, by Eugène Grasset

June: The Sixth Month

And what is so rare as a day in June?
Then, if ever, come perfect days;
Then Heaven tries earth if it be in tune,
And over it softly her warm ear lays.

— *James Russell Lowell*

In the Julian and Gregorian calendars, June is the sixth month of the year. It's one of the four months that have only 30 days. No months start on the same day of the week as June, an oddity shared only by May. However, June ends on the same day of the week as March in both common and leap years.

In the Northern Hemisphere, June is the month with the longest daylight hours; in the Southern Hemisphere, it's the one with the shortest, equivalent to December. The meteorological summer begins June 21 (the Summer Solstice) in the Northern Hemisphere; the meteorological winter begins on the same day in the Southern Hemisphere (the Winter Solstice).

The English name of June takes its name from the Latin *Iunius*. The poet Ovid gives two theories for the origin of the name. The first is that June is named for the Roman goddess Juno, wife of Jupiter and queen of the gods. The second is that the name comes from the Latin word *iuniores* ("younger ones"), and that the previous month of May comes from *maiores* ("elders")

As the early Roman calendar started its new year in March, June was originally the fourth month of the year. It's uncertain when the Romans switched the new year to January, but it may have been as late as 153 BCE.

June, George Auriol

June in Other Cultures

The month of June has different names in different languages. Some nations use calendars other than the Gregorian, and their months may overlap with June. In lunar-based calendars, such as Islam, months move through the seasons, but they often have a word for June itself.

Albanian: Qershor
Arabic (Egyptian, Sudanese, Moroccan): يونيو (*yūniyū*)
Arabic (Levantine): حزيران (*ḥuzayrān*)
Arabic (Libyan): الصيف (*al-sayf*)
Arabic (Algerian): جوان (*Juwān*)
Azerbaijani: İyun
Basque: Ekain

Bulgarian: юни (*juni*)

Chinese: 六月 (Cantonese: *luhkyuht*; Mandarin: *liùyuè*; Taiwanese: *lak-goeh*)

Corsican: Chjugnu

Czech: červen

Finnish: Kesäkuu

French: Juin

German, Norwegian: Juni

Greek: Ιούνιος (*Ioúnios*)

Hebrew: יוני (*yûnî*)

Hindi: जून (*jūn*)

Hungarian: Június

Irish (Gaelic): Meitheamh mí an Mheithimh

Italian: Giugno

Japanese (traditional calendar): 六月 (*rokugatsu*); 水無月 (*minaduki*)

Korean: 유월 (*yuweol*)

Lithuanian: Birželis

Maori: Pipiri

Old English: Sēremōnaþ

Polish: Czerwiec

Russian: июнь (*ijun'*)

Sesotho: Phupjane

Spanish: Junio

Swedish, Swahili: Juni

Thai: Mithunayon

Vietnamese: 腑𢀭 (tháng sáu)

Welsh: Mehefin

June Brides (and Other Sayings and Superstitions)

June is the most popular month for weddings, followed by August. There are a number of sayings and superstitions about June brides and June weddings.

> "A June bride is joyful, jubilant, and jolly well jovial."

> "A June bride will be impetuous, and generous."

> "Married in the month of roses (June), life will be one long honeymoon."

> "Marry when June roses grow, over land and sea you'll go."

> "When you marry in June, you'll be a bride all your life." (from the song *June Bride*.)

Which day to get married? That's easy. "Monday for wealth, Tuesday for health, Wednesday the best day of all, Thursday for losses, Friday for crosses, Saturday for no luck at all."

Why such an emphasis on June? Some say it's in honor of Juno, the goddess of marriage. Others suggest it's because back in Medieval days, people would usually have their (yes) annual bath in May, so they'd still be relatively fresh by June. This may also explain the custom of the bridal bouquet.

According to superstition, May is the most unlucky month for marriages, but in ancient Rome the "inauspicious" period ran from May 15 to June 15. The high priestess of Jupiter told the poet Ovid to delay his daughter's wedding until after that date.

There are also some June proverbs for farmers.

"A calm June puts the farmer in tune."

"June damp and warm, does the farmer no harm."

June Symbols

Birthstone Pearl, moonstone, or alexandrite.

Pearl

Moonstone

Alexandrite

Birth Flowers Rose and Honeysuckle

Roses, by Vincent van Gogh

Honeysuckle

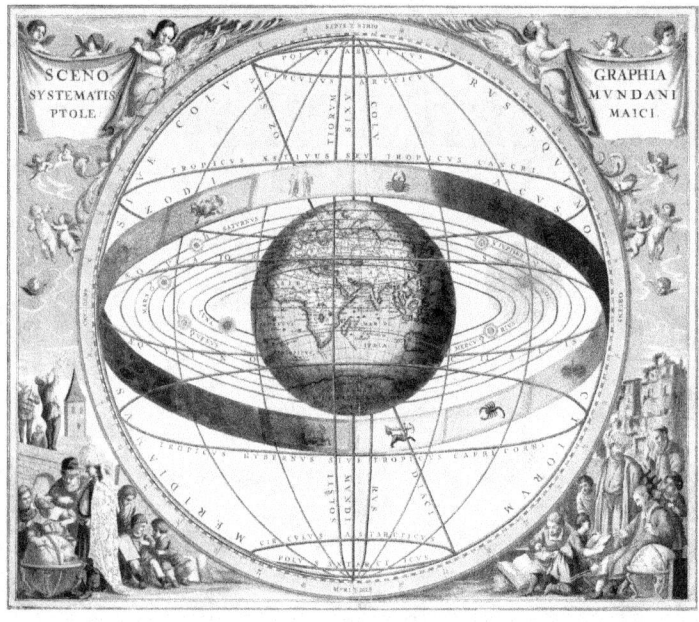

Scenography of the Ptolemaic Cosmography, by Johannes van Loon, based on Andreas Cellarius's *Harmonia Macrocosmica,* 1660

June 18 Zodiac Signs

From the perspective of someone on Earth, the Sun appears to move through the sky throughout the year, along a path astronomers call the *ecliptic plane*. The ecliptic plane is divided into twelve constellations, known as the zodiac, based on traditionally observed patterns of stars. On your birthday, you can't see your constellation, because it's in the daytime sky.

The zodiac was first developed by Babylonian astronomers about 2,500 years ago. Because they were unaware that the Earth wobbles like a spinning top (known as *precession*), they didn't make allowance for the fact that the Sun's path through the zodiac changes over time.

That means there are now two sets of dates for your birth sign. The *tropical dates* are the original Babylonian dates; the *sidereal dates* tell you where the Sun actually appears as it moves along its annual path.

June 18, however, is one of the few days of the year in which the tropical sign and the sidereal sign are the same: **Gemini.**

Gemini

Tropical May 22 to June 21
Sidereal June 16 to July 15

According to Greek mythology, Leda, wife of the King of Sparta, gave birth to Helen of Troy and Clytemnestra. The god Zeus, disguised as a swan, seduced her after she had already lain with her husband on the same night. This resulted in two eggs, which hatched to become the twins Castor and Pollux. Castor's father was the King of Sparta, but Pollux was the son of Zeus and therefore immortal. When Castor died, Pollux shared his immortality, so that they could divide their time between Hades and Olympus. They were enshrined in the Zodiac as the constellation Gemini, the Twins.

In astrology, Gemini is an air sign, ruled by Mercury, compatible with Libra, Aquarius, and Aries. Geminis are supposed to be communicative, flexible, intellectual, and curious, but prone to fickleness and easily distracted.

The Sign of Gemini, by Giovanni Maria Falconetto (Courtesy
Palazzo d'Arco, Mantua, Italy)

Illustration by Edward Penfield

What Day of the Week is June 18?

On what day of the week does June 18 fall?

Surprisingly, this isn't an easy question. Because the calendar year is 365 days long (366 in leap years), it doesn't divide evenly by the seven days of the week.

Also, the Earth goes around the Sun in about 365-1/4 days, so a calendar tends to drift over time. That's why the same date falls on different weekdays in different years.

This is made even more complicated by a change in calendars that took place in 1582. Our modern calendar has its roots in ancient Rome, in a calendar reform conducted by Julius Caesar. Caesar commissioned mathematicians to attack the problem, and they came up with the idea of leap years, and thus standardized the calendar for centuries to come. This was called the Julian calendar.

Over time, however, the small errors in Caesar's calculation compounded. That's why Pope Gregory XIII commissioned the Gregorian calendar, used in most of the world today. Some countries converted in 1582, when the calendar was first developed; some converted later; other still haven't changed.

Gregorian and Julian aren't the only types of calendars. The Hebrew year, the Islamic year, and many other calendars are used in different parts of the world and among different people.

You can convert Gregorian dates to other calendars, including the Hebrew calendar, the Islamic calendar, and even the Mayan calendar by visiting the Fourmilab Calendar Converter at http://www.fourmilab.ch/documents/calendar/.

Chinese calendar systems are quite complex and have changed several times; a full discussion is far beyond the scope of this book. If you're interested, you can find information here: http://www.hermetic.ch/cal_stud/chinese_cal.htm.

On Names and Dates

Historians use "CE" (Common Era) and "BCE" (Before the Common Era) instead of the more common "AD" (Anno Domini, or Year of Our Lord) and "BC" (Before Christ), reflecting the fact that the year-numbering system established by the Gregorian calendar is used throughout the world in many countries not culturally Christian.

The CE/BCE designation dates back to at least 1708, and has been adopted as a standard by the United Nations and the Universal Postal Union. Because this series of books covers events and people of all nations and cultures, we use the CE/BCE terms.

The abbreviation "O.S." ("Old Style") and "N.S." ("New Style") on some dates refers to the fact that the Russian Empire (in particular) did not switch from the Julian to the Gregorian calendar at the same time as the rest of Europe, and therefore some figures and events have two dates.

Also, in the Julian calendar in England in the 16th century, the year began on March 25 rather than January 1. To avoid confusion with Gregorian dates, dates between January and March were often written using both years.

People and events whose original names are not in the Western alphabet have their native names (where possible) in the appropriate script shown in parenthesis. If you are using an e-reader to access an electronic version of this book, all characters don't always display on all devices.

A 50-year brass perpetual calendar.

Quote of the Day

"Time is an illusion, lunchtime doubly so."

Douglas Adams,
from *The Hitchhiker's Guide to the Galaxy*

Notes
and
Credits

THEM ACC MAGNA

Timespinner Press

Cartoon by John T. McCutcheon

Copyright, Credit, and Contact

Follow Us

Our blog "This Day in History" (http://
timespinnerpress.com/this-day-in-history/) features short
articles on events and people associated with each day, and
updates several times each week. Also subscribe to the
"Quote of the Day" at http://timespinnerpress.com/quote-
of-the-day/. You can get daily links by following us on
Facebook at TimespinnerPress, or on Twitter as
@sidewisethinker.

Contact Us

Find an error or a format problem? Want information about
the series, about us, or about when the volume for your
special day might be available? Please email us at
editor@timespinnerpress.com. (We also take requests if your
special day isn't yet complete. Please give us at least six
weeks' notice if possible.)

Sources

We owe a great debt to Wikipedia, which is our first stop for
research. We attempt to make independent confirmation of
all important dates and facts through a variety of other
sources.

Other sources we frequently use include the Library of
Congress; "on this day" listings from *Encyclopedia Britannica*,
the *New York Times*, and the BBC; Omniglot for the names of
months in other languages; *Chase's Calendar of Events*; and, of
course, the always essential Google.

All art and photographs are either in the public domain, used under a Creative Commons license, or with a "fair use" justification, and most frequently come from Wikimedia Commons and the Library of Congress Prints and Photographs Division.

Attribution is provided where possible, or as requested by the copyright owner, or when there is particular historical significance, listed below. For information about any particular illustration or photograph, please contact us.

Credits

1. The cover painting of the Battle of Waterloo by Thomas Jones Barker was created prior to 1882, and is in the public domain because its copyright has expired.

2. The illustration of the month of June used on the back cover is from the French Gothic illuminated manuscript *Les Très Riches Heures du duc de Berry* by the Limbourg Brothers, Jean Colombe, and an intermediate painter whose name is lost to history. It is in the public domain because its copyright has expired.

3. The box graphic used on the first page is from a 1916 pamphlet entitled "Divorce versus Democracy" authored by G. K. Chesterton, originally published in London by the Society of St. Peter and St. Paul. It is in the public domain in the US because it was published prior to 1923, and is in the public domain in all countries (including the country of origin) in which the copyright time is the author's life plus 70 years or less.

4. The graphic design for the section pages in this book is from a design originally created for a pharmacy label. It is courtesy of Wellcome Images (ICV No 11073, photo V0010813), and is used here under CC BY-SA 4.0.

5. The portrait of Napoleon Bonaparte was painted circa 1840 by Paul Delaroche, and is in the public domain because its copyright has expired. The image is courtesy Library of Congress, digital ID cph.3c17921.

6. The portrait of Arthur Wellesley, 1st Duke of Wellington, was painted by Thomas Lawrence in 1815, and is in the public domain because its copyright has expired. The painting is part of the Royal Collection, Windsor Castle.

7. The painting of Gebhard Leberecht von Blücher was created circa 1815 by an unknown artist copying an earlier painting by Paul Ernst Gebauer. It is in the public domain because its copyright has expired.

8. The map of the Battle of Waterloo is taken from the book *Battles of the Nineteenth Century*, by Archibald Forbes and A. Hilliard Atteridge (New York: Cassell and Company), originally published in 1901. It is in the public domain because its copyright has expired.

9. The photograph of Amelia Earhart prior to her 1928 transatlantic flight was taken for Wide World Photos. It is in the public domain because no evidence of a copyright filing has been found and it was first published in the United States between 1923 and 1977 without a copyright notice.

10. The 1983 photograph of Sally Ride is in the public domain as a work created by an employee of NASA as part of that person's official duties. It is courtesy NASA, photo ID GPN-2000-001081.

11. The 1942 photograph of Sir Winston Churchill is in the public domain as a work created by an employee of the US Office of War Information as part of that person's official duties. It is courtesy of the Library of Congress, digital ID fsa.8e00870.

12. The 1964 photograph of Paul McCartney with the Beatles playing for the Dutch television network VARA is courtesy of the Beeld en Geluid Wiki under the CC BY-SA 3.0 Netherlands license. It is catalog number 64228 kb, photograph number 39. The photograph has been cropped.

13. The 1917 "Uncle Sam Wants You" poster by James Montgomery Flagg is courtesy Library of Congress, LC-USZC2-564, digital ID cph.3b48465. It is in the public domain both as a work created by a contract employee for the US federal government as part of that person's contracted duties, and because it was first published prior to January 1, 1923. This version has been restored digitally from the original image.

14. The 1914 photograph of Grand Duchesses Anastasia and Maria is in the public domain in Russia according to article 1256 of Book IV of the Civil Code of the Russian Federation No. 230-FZ of December 18, 2006. It was published on territory of the Russian Empire or Republic before November 7, 1917, and was not republished for 30 days following on the territory of the Soviet Union or any other states. It is in the public domain in the United States because it was published prior to January 1, 1923.

15. The 1970 photograph of Roger Ebert was cropped from a photograph of Ebert with Russ Meyer. The original photograph was donated by Roger Ebert and is used here under the CC BY-SA 3.0 license.

16. The 1962 CBS publicity photograph from *Have Gun — Will Travel* is in the public domain because it was published in the United States between 1923 and 1977 without a copyright notice. Traditionally, publicity photographs are not copyrighted because of the way in which they are intended to be used.

17. The 1936 lobby card from the film *San Francisco* is in the public domain because it was published in the United States between 1923 and 1977 without a copyright notice.

18. The 1938 poster from the film *Tarzan's Revenge* is in the public domain because it was published in the United States between 1923 and 1977 without a copyright notice.

19. The 1899 photograph of Roald Amundsen was taken by Daniel Georg Nyblin and is courtesy of the National Library of Norway. Although the photograph is in the public domain because its copyright has expired, the image carries the CC BY-SA 2.0 license.

20. The photograph of Max Immelmann was taken in 1916 or earlier and is in the public domain because its copyright has expired. It is courtesy of the Great War Primary Documents Archive.

21. The 1850s illustration of the Ranee *(sic)* of Jhansi is in the public domain because its copyright has expired.

22. The 2009 photograph of Clarence Clemons with the E Street Band in Baltimore during the Wrecking Ball Tour was taken

by Jamison Foser, and is used here under CC BY-SA 2.0. It has been cropped.

23. The 1951 Bowman Gum trading card of Larry Doby is in the public domain because it was published in the United States between 1923 and 1963, and although there may or may not have been a copyright notice, the copyright was not renewed.

24. The 1940 poster for a father and son banquet sponsored by the Chicago Urban League was created by Albert M. Bender. It is from the Works Projects Administration Poster Collection in the Library of Congress, digital ID cph. 3b48794. It is in the public domain as a work created by an employee of the US government as part of that person's official duties.

25. The 2008 photograph of the Trooping of the Color was taken by "Ibagli," who released the work into the public domain without restrictions. It has been cropped.

26. The 1946 photograph of Sarah Vaughn was taken by William P. Gottlieb, and is part of the William P. Gottlieb Collection of jazz photographs at the Library of Congress. In accordance with the wishes of Gottlieb, the photographs in the collection entered into the public domain in 2010.

27. The 1847 painting *The Happy Moment* by James Goodwyn Clonney is in the public domain because its copyright has expired. The painting can be found in the Museum of Fine Arts, Boston, accession number 47.1222.

28. The 2006 photograph of a martini was taken by Hayford Peirce, who released the work into the public domain without restrictions.

29. The 1896 drawing "June" by Eugène Grasset is in the public domain because its copyright has expired.

30. The 1912 graphic of June by George Auriol is in the public domain because its copyright has expired.

31. The 1815 woodcut of a proposal is in the public domain because its copyright has expired.

32. The photo of a pearl necklace is by "Anna reg," taken from Wikimedia Commons and used here under CC BY-SA 3.0.

33. The photograph of a Brazilian moonstone is by Didier Descouens, taken from Wikimedia Commons and used here under CC BY-SA 4.0.

34. The photograph of alexandrite under ultraviolet light is by Parent Géry, taken from Wikimedia Commons and used here because the creator has dedicated the rights to the public domain under CC0 1.0.

35. The painting *Roses* by Vincent Van Gogh can be found in the collection of the National Gallery of Art, Washington, DC. The image is in the public domain because its copyright has expired.

36. The illustration of honeysuckle originally appeared in the book *American Homes and Gardens*, published by Munn & Co., New York, in 1905. It is in the public domain because its copyright has expired. The image was taken from Flickr's The Commons.

37. The celestial sphere is from *Scenography of the Ptolemaic Cosmography*, by Johannes van Loon, based on Andreas Cellarius's *Harmonia Macrocosmica*, 1660. It is in the public domain because its copyright has expired.

38. The fresco *The Sign of Gemini* was created between 1515 and 1520 by Giovanni Maria Falconetto, and is in the public domain because its copyright has expired. It is located in the Palazzo d'Arco, Mantua, Italy.

39. The 1906 automobile calendar is by Edward Penfield, and is in the collection of the Library of Congress Prints and Photographs Division. It is in the public domain because its copyright has expired.

40. The 50-year perpetual calendar photograph is in the public domain.

41. The painting "June" is from the *Brevarium Grimani,* circa 1510, and is in the public domain because its copyright has expired.

License Description and Terms

Aside from material purely in the public domain, photographs and other material in this book are used under specific licenses permitting free use, usually with an attribution requirement. For full text and terms of these licenses, click or enter the appropriate links below. If you believe there is an error in the copyright status or attribution of any of these images, please email us.

- Creative Commons Attribution 2.0 Generic (CC-BY 2.0): http://creativecommons.org/licenses/by/2.0/deed.en
- Creative Commons Attribution-Share Alike 3.0 Generic (CC-BY-SA 3.0): http://creativecommons.org/licenses/by-sa/3.0/
- Creative Commons Attribution-Share Alike 2.5 Generic (CC-BY-SA 2.5): http://creativecommons.org/licenses/by-sa/2.5/deed.en
- Creative Commons Attribution-Share Alike 2.0 Generic (CC-BY-SA 2.0): http://creativecommons.org/licenses/by/2.0/deed.en
- Creative Commons Attribution-Share Alike 1.0 Generic (CC-BY-SA 1.0): http://creativecommons.org/licenses/by-sa/1.0/deed.en
- CC0 1.0 Universal (CC0 1.0) Public Domain Dedication (CC0 1.0) http://creativecommons.org/publicdomain/zero/1.0/deed.en
- GNU Free Documentation License (GFDL): http://en.wikipedia.org/wiki/Wikipedia:Text_of_the_GNU_Free_Documentation_License
- License Art Libre (Free Art License): http://artlibre.org

Timespinner
Press

"June," from the *Brevarium Grimani* by Simon Bening (c.1510)

Other Books from Timespinner Press

The Story of a Special Day
Michael Dobson

A series of (eventually) 366 volumes covering everything that happened on your special day! Events, births, deaths, quotes, holidays, and much more. It's like a birthday card they'll never throw away!

US$7.95 print/US$2.99 ebook.

From Plassey to Pakistan
Humayun Mirza

The history of British Colonial India and the formation of Pakistan from the unique perspective of the son of Pakistan's first president and last of the royal line of Bengal, Bihar, and Orissa! This unique historical document tells the inside story of this distinguished family, including the detailed story of the coup that toppled his father from power!

US$27.95 print

A Whole New Navy: America's War in the Pacific

Miles Durr

The most comprehensive and detailed description of America's naval war in the Pacific ever—every battle, every ship, every task force and every task group from Pearl Harbor through the Japanese surrender! A must-have for the collection of every World War II buff!

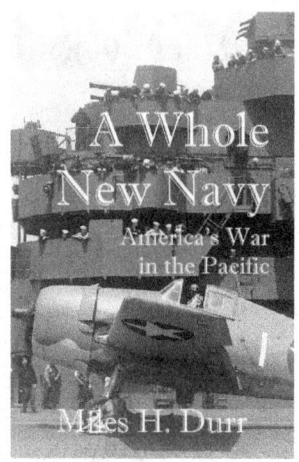

US$29.95 print

Improbable History: The Weird, the Obscure, and the Strangely Important

edited by Michael Dobson

From the birth of Western civilization to the rescue of Apollo 13, from the Leaning Tower of Pisa to Florence's Duomo, history has often turned on small, improbable details. Whatever happened to the ancient Samaritan people? Why did a fortuitous rainstorm allow the British to conquer India? How did an air raid in Italy lead to the development of chemotherapy? What happened when Albert Einstein met Adolf Hitler on the streets of Berlin? How did the Japanese manage to attack the US mainland using balloons? A cast of award-winning writers tackle some of the strangest tales in history!

US$19.95 print

www.ingramcontent.com/pod-product-compliance
Lightning Source LLC
Chambersburg PA
CBHW060201290526
45789CB00003B/1117